The 21st Century Millionaire

Modern Strategies for Building Wealth

Andrew Galowey

Copyright © [Andrew Galowey] [2024]. All rights reserved. No part of this publication may be reproduced, distributed, or transmitted in any form or by any means, including photocopying, recording, or other electronic or mechanical methods, without the prior written permission of the publisher, except in the case of brief quotations embodied in critical reviews and certain other noncommercial uses permitted by copyright law.

Table Of Contents

Introduction

Chapter 1: Shifting Sands: The Changing Landscape of Wealth Building

Chapter 2: Foundations First: The Cornerstones of a Safe Future

Chapter 3: Beyond Brick and Mortar: Modern Perspectives on Real Estate Investment

Chapter 4: The Robo-Revolution: Leveraging Technology for Smarter Investing

Chapter 5: Cryptocurrency: Navigating the New Frontier (Responsibly)

Conclusion

Introduction

The conventional route to wealth creation - a stable employment, a diverse portfolio of stocks and bonds, and a physical property - is no longer the only way to succeed. Welcome to the twenty-first century, when financial innovation and technology upheaval have created a wealth of new options. This book, "The 21st Century Millionaire: Modern Strategies for Building Wealth," will help you navigate this fascinating, yet sometimes complicated, terrain.

In these pages, we will look at how the financial game has altered. We'll clarify common misconceptions and expose you to cutting-edge solutions such as robo-advisors and real estate crowdfunding. We won't forget the tried-and-true strategies, which will provide you with a firm basis for your wealth-building path. But, most significantly, we'll highlight prudent investment, which is critical in today's changing market. Whether you're an experienced investor or just getting started, "The 21st Century Millionaire" will provide you with the information and methods you need to become a financial powerhouse in today's world.

Chapter 1: Shifting Sands: The Changing Landscape of Wealth Building

The promise of financial stability has long driven the American Dream, which includes a comfortable house, a secure future, and the flexibility to follow your hobbies. Traditionally, realizing this ideal required a stable career, a diverse portfolio of stocks and bonds, and maybe a rental property or two. It was a gradual and steady ascent, based on patience and measured risks.

However, the twenty-first century has brought forth a financial environment that our parents and grandparents could never have envisioned. Technological improvements have transformed how we invest, manage our money, and even own property. The internet has democratized access to financial information, and new technologies such as robo-advisors and real estate crowdfunding have made previously inaccessible investment options possible.

So, what does this imply for today's aspiring millionaires? Is it necessary to toss aside the old playbook entirely? Not exactly. While the means and tactics have developed, the fundamental principles of ethical wealth creation remain unchanged. This chapter will look at the changing sands of the financial world, including how the conventional model is being challenged, what new possibilities are developing, and why responding to these changes is critical for financial success in the twenty-first century.

Cracks in the foundation

The old approach to wealth growth, although dependable, had limits. It often needed a considerable initial investment, making it less accessible to individuals starting out with modest funds. Furthermore, people who lack financial knowledge may find it difficult to navigate the complexity of the stock market and real estate.

Furthermore, the economic realities of the twenty-first century have placed pressure on the old paradigm. Many people are finding it more difficult to save for a down payment or invest in a diverse portfolio due to stagnant salaries, rising living expenses, and student loan debt. These are the exact conditions that have spurred the hunt for new routes of wealth acquisition.

The Rise of FinTech Revolution

The internet has made financial information and services more accessible than ever before. This has enabled people to take a more active part in managing their money. A variety of internet services include financial education, investment research tools, and budgeting programs.

Fintech (financial technology) is leading the way in this transformation. Fintech businesses use cutting-edge technology to challenge the conventional banking industry. They provide new goods and services that are more accessible, cost-effective, and user-friendly than their physical equivalents.

New Kids on the Block: Robo-Advisors and Crowdfunding

One of the most interesting trends in finance is the growth of robo-advisors. These automated investing platforms employ algorithms to generate and maintain diverse portfolios depending on your specific financial objectives and risk tolerance. Robo-consultants often offer cheaper costs than conventional financial advisors, making them more accessible to more investors.

Real estate crowdfunding platforms have also provided access to a formerly restricted asset class. These platforms enable people to invest in real estate projects with modest amounts of money. This provides an alternative to the high initial expenditures associated with conventional real estate investing, enabling more individuals to benefit from the potential returns of the property market.

Cryptocurrency: A Double-edged Sword

The rise of cryptocurrencies, such as Bitcoin, has further blurred the limits of conventional banking. Although the potential rewards are large, the market remains very volatile and speculative. This makes it a dangerous prospect for most investors, emphasizing the significance of thorough study and appropriate behavior.

Adapting and thriving

The twenty-first century provides both obstacles and opportunity for wealth creation. The key to success is to recognize these changes and adjust your financial plan appropriately. This does not imply forsaking the fundamental concepts of diversification and smart investment. Rather, it necessitates an openness to new tools and methods that might supplement your conventional portfolio and expedite your journey to financial independence.

The next chapters of this book will dive further into these new wealth-building instruments, explain the risks and benefits, and show you how to incorporate them into a smart investing plan. We'll also go over the basic concepts of wealth creation and provide you with the information and skills needed to manage the ever-changing financial world.

So tighten your seatbelts, because we're about to go on a trip to generate riches in the thrilling but challenging world of the 21st century billionaire.

Chapter 2: Foundations First: The Cornerstones of a Safe Future

While the twenty-first century presents a wealth of interesting investing options, establishing a sound financial foundation remains critical. Regardless of the instruments you choose, a solid foundation of appropriate financial practices will guarantee that your wealth-building path is both sustainable and safe. This chapter revisits the fundamental ideas that underpin financial well-being in the contemporary world.

Building a Budget: Your Financial Roadmap

The foundation of every effective financial strategy is a well-defined budget. A budget serves as a road map, enabling you to manage your income and spending while ensuring you're living within your means. Popular budgeting approaches, such as the 50/30/20 rule (which allocates 50% of income to necessities, 30% to desires, and 20% to savings and debt reduction), provide a decent beginning point.

Taming the Beast: Strategic Debt Management

Debt isn't always terrible. Mortgages, for example, may be an effective strategy for accumulating wealth. However, if debt is not managed properly, it may soon become a financial burden that limits your capacity to save and invest.

There are two basic methods for efficiently managing debt. The first step is to prioritize high-interest debt, such as credit card debt, and work on paying it down first. The second option uses the snowball or avalanche method. The snowball strategy involves paying off the lowest debts first, regardless of interest rate, and gathering momentum as you erase them. The avalanche strategy emphasizes repaying loans with the highest interest rates first, which saves you money in the long term.

Building Your Safety Net: The Emergency Fund

Life is full of unexpected occurrences, such as automobile maintenance and medical problems. An emergency fund offers a financial cushion to help you weather these storms without jeopardizing your long-term ambitions. Aim to save 3-6 months' worth of living costs in an easily accessible account.

The Power of Compound Interest: Start Saving Early

Albert Einstein famously described compound interest as "the eighth wonder of the world." This theory permits your money to increase exponentially over time. The sooner you begin saving and investing, the longer your money has to profit from compound interest. Even tiny sums saved regularly might have a big influence in the long run.

Embrace Automation: Set Up Your Savings System

Automating your savings and bill payments is an effective approach to keep on track toward your financial objectives. Schedule automatic transfers from your checking account to your savings and investment accounts. This eliminates the desire to squander the money, ensuring that your savings increase gradually.

The Power of "No": Controlling Impulse Purchases

Impulse buying is a typical financial problem. Before buying a non-essential purchase, consider if it corresponds with your financial objectives. Could you live without it? Implementing a "cooling-off period" between viewing an item and purchasing it may assist to reduce impulsive spending.

Insurance: Protecting Your Assets

Having enough insurance protects your assets and future earning potential. Health insurance protects you against unexpected medical expenses, while disability insurance offers financial stability if you are unable to work due to sickness or accident. Life insurance guarantees that your loved ones are financially secure in the event that you die.

Embrace continuous learning

The financial environment is continuously changing. Commit to becoming a lifelong student in personal finance. Read books, listen to podcasts, and take online courses to remain up to date on new investing prospects and methods.

The ideas covered in this chapter may seem simple, yet they are essential for every effective wealth-building plan. You may lay a strong financial foundation by creating a budget, managing debt responsibly, setting up an emergency fund, and saving regularly. The new tools and tactics discussed in later chapters will build on this foundation, hastening your path to becoming a 21st-century billionaire. Remember that financial success is a marathon, not a sprint. By adhering to these key concepts, you'll be well on your way to accomplishing your financial objectives and creating a secure future.

Chapter 3: Beyond Brick and Mortar: Modern Perspectives on Real Estate Investment

Real estate has traditionally been a source of wealth creation. Historically, investing in real estate included owning a home to either live in or rent out to renters. While this technique is still effective, the twenty-first century provides a wealth of new opportunities for becoming engaged in the real estate market, typically with fewer upfront expenditures and more flexibility. This chapter delves into current approaches to real estate investing, enabling you to include this asset class into your wealth-building plan.

The Classics Revisited: Buying and Renting Properties

Buying a rental property may be a profitable method to earn passive income and accumulate long-term wealth. Rental revenue provides consistent cash flow, while the property itself might increase in value over time. However, this strategy necessitates a considerable initial investment for a down payment as well as recurring costs for upkeep, repairs, and property management.

House Flipping is a high-risk, high-reward strategy

House flipping is purchasing a house that requires renovation, fixing it up, and then selling it for a profit. This strategy may be very successful, but it also has major dangers. Accurately forecasting remodeling costs, market swings, and holding durations is critical to success. House flipping requires substantial knowledge of construction, real estate trends, and market research.

REITs: Owning a Piece of the Real Estate Pie

REITs provide a more passive option to invest in real estate. REITs are businesses that hold and manage income-generating real estate assets. By investing in a REIT, you effectively own a portion of a diverse portfolio of real estate assets. REITs trade on stock markets alongside other securities, making them a highly liquid investment. Furthermore, REITs are obligated to transfer a considerable percentage of their taxable revenue to shareholders, ensuring a consistent source of income.

Real Estate Crowdfunding: Democratizing Access

Real estate crowdfunding platforms have transformed how people invest in real estate. These platforms enable investors to combine their funds and finance real estate projects with modest quantities of money. This opens up a previously inaccessible asset class, making real estate investing more accessible to a broader spectrum of people. However, real estate crowdfunding is still a relatively young and uncontrolled business. Before making an investment, thoroughly examine the platform, project sponsor, and underlying property.

Real Estate Investment Platforms: Hands-Off Approach

Real estate investment platforms bring together investors and developers looking for capital for commercial or residential projects. Investors may choose between loan and equity interests in these ventures. Debt investments provide a set rate of return, while equity holdings have the potential for higher gains but also involve more risk. These platforms provide a more hands-off approach to real estate investment than conventional approaches such as purchasing and renting property. However, similar to real estate crowdfunding, comprehensive due research is required before investing.

Choosing the Right Approach

The optimal real estate investing strategy for you is determined by your specific financial objectives, risk tolerance, and desired degree of engagement.

For individuals looking for passive income and diversity, REITs may be a suitable option.
- House flipping may be a viable choice for investors with a greater risk tolerance and expertise in remodeling and building.
- Real estate crowdfunding platforms provide options for people with low funds but a desire to participate more actively.
- Real estate investing platforms may be of interest to investors who want a hands-off approach yet are willing to take on a greater risk profile.

Importance of Location and Market Research

Regardless of the technique you use, location remains an important consideration in real estate investing. Investigate the individual market, including rental patterns, vacancy rates, and property appreciation prospects.

The Power of Professional Advice

Consulting a knowledgeable real estate specialist is strongly advised, particularly for first-time investors. They can assist you in navigating the complexities of the market, identifying acceptable investment possibilities, and ensuring that your selections are consistent with your overall financial objectives.

Real estate remains a potent instrument for wealth creation in the twenty-first century. In comparison to previous approaches, the contemporary solutions discussed in this chapter provide more flexibility, accessibility, and variety. By carefully examining your risk tolerance, financial objectives, and desired degree of engagement, you may choose the real estate investing strategy that best meets your requirements and accelerates you toward becoming a 21st-century billionaire.

Chapter 4: The Robo-Revolution: Leveraging Technology for Smarter Investing

The financial environment may be overwhelming, particularly for people with little past expertise. Sifting through piles of financial data, studying market patterns, and building a diverse portfolio might seem intimidating. This is where robo-acvisors enter the picture.

Robo-Revolution: Automating Your Investment Journey

Robo-advisors are digital platforms that use algorithms to provice automated investing advice and portfolio management. They often appeal to a wide variety of investors, from total novices to those who want a hands-off approach to investment management.

How Robo Advisors Work

Getting started with a robo-advisor is a straightforward procedure. The platform uses an online questionnaire to analyze your financial condition, risk tolerance, and investing objectives. Based on your responses, the robo-advisor offers a bespoke investment strategy made up of low-cost exchange-traded funds (ETFs). These ETFs provide diversity across asset types, which reduces risk and aligns with your long-term objectives.

Advantages of Robo-Advisors

There are numerous compelling reasons to use a robo-advisor in your wealth-building strategy:

- Accessibility and Affordability: Robo-advisers often have lower minimum investment requirements than conventional financial advisors, making them available to a broader spectrum of investors. Furthermore,

their costs are often substantially cheaper, giving them an affordable option for portfolio management.
- Convenience and Automation: Robo-advisors provide a user-friendly platform for monitoring portfolio performance, adjusting risk tolerance, and rebalancing holdings - all from the comfort of your own home. They automate operations like as rebalancing, ensuring that your portfolio remains aligned with your objectives even when market circumstances change.
- Discipline and Emotionless Investing: Human emotions may often muddle investing decisions, resulting in rash actions that might derail your financial strategy. Robo-advisors exclude emotions from the equation by adopting a predetermined plan based on your risk tolerance and long-term objectives.

- Diversification and Risk Management: Robo-advisors often build portfolios using low-cost ETFs, which naturally diversify across asset classes. This diversity reduces risk and smoothes market volatility, safeguarding your wealth.

Are Robo-Advisors Right For You?

While robo-advisors provide several benefits, they may not be ideal for everyone.

- Limited Investment possibilities: Robo-advisors often provide a pre-defined range of investment possibilities, which may not be suitable for investors seeking very specific investing plans. A conventional financial adviser may be a better choice for folks with sophisticated financial requirements or who want greater control over their particular assets.

Robo-advisors provide little human involvement. While most platforms include customer service agents, they may not give the same degree of individualized advice and assistance as a conventional financial adviser.

Selecting the Right Robo-Advisor

The robo-advisor industry is continuously changing, with several platforms competing for your business. Here are some important considerations to consider before making your decision:

- Minimum Investment: Determine the platform's minimum investment requirements. Some appeal to new investors with lower minimums, while others target existing investors with bigger portfolios.
- Investment Strategy: Research the many investment alternatives provided by the robo-advisor. Check if their

mindset is compatible with your risk tolerance and financial objectives.
- Fees: Compare the fees levied by various sites. These prices might vary greatly, so selecting a cost-effective alternative is critical.
- Account Features: Consider the platform's features, such as automatic rebalancing, tax-loss harvesting (selling assets at a loss to reduce capital gains taxes), and mobile app access.

Robo-advisors are an effective tool for the 21st century investor. They provide a simple, cost-effective, and automated approach to develop and manage your portfolio. While they may not be the best choice for everyone, robo-advisors make complicated investing methods more accessible and may be an invaluable tool in your wealth-building path. You may use robo-advisors to reach your financial objectives by recognizing their benefits and limits, as well as carefully selecting the correct platform.

Chapter 5: Cryptocurrency: Navigating the New Frontier (Responsibly)

Cryptocurrency has grown in popularity over the last several years. Bitcoin, the first and best-known cryptocurrency, has made headlines for its dramatic price fluctuations and promise of massive rewards. This chapter digs into the complicated world of cryptocurrencies, discussing its potential rewards and pitfalls while highlighting the significance of ethical investment in this new asset class.

Demystifying cryptocurrency:

Cryptocurrency, or crypto for short, is a digital money that uses cryptography for security. Unlike conventional currencies regulated by governments, Bitcoin is based on a decentralized technology called blockchain. Blockchain is a digital log of transactions that is spread over a network of computers, making it secure and transparent.

The allure of cryptocurrency:

Several causes are driving the increase in bitcoin adoption:

- Decentralization: Cryptocurrencies work independently of conventional financial institutions, giving you more autonomy and control over your funds.

- Potential for High Returns: In the early days of Bitcoin, several investors made big returns. However, keep in mind that these returns come with a significant level of volatility.

- Borderless Transactions: Cryptocurrencies enable rapid and low-cost international transactions by avoiding conventional banking costs.

- Innovation and promise: The underlying blockchain technology has enormous promise for uses outside money, including as secure data storage and smart contracts.

Risks to Consider:

Despite its attraction, Bitcoin remains a difficult and dangerous financial option. Here are some important considerations:

- Volatility: The cryptocurrency market is very volatile, which means that values may move substantially in a short time. Due to its volatility, it is a dangerous investment for people looking for consistency and predictable returns.

- Regulation: The regulatory environment for cryptocurrencies is continually changing. This ambiguity may be risky for investors, since governments may impose tighter laws in the future.

- Security Risks: Cryptocurrency exchanges and wallets are subject to hacker attempts, which may result in the loss of your investment. It is vital that you store your bitcoin safely.

- Limited use: Although bitcoin use is increasing, it is still not commonly recognized as a means of payment. This restricts its practical use and may impede its future development.

Responsible cryptocurrency investing:

If you're thinking about investing in bitcoin, it's important to do so wisely.

- Do Your Research: Before investing in any cryptocurrency, learn about its technology, purpose, and possible dangers and benefits.

- Start little: Due to the extreme volatility of cryptocurrencies, invest just a little amount of your capital that you can afford to lose.

- Diversify Your Portfolio: Avoid putting all your eggs in one basket. Cryptocurrency should only make up a modest portion of a well-diversified investing portfolio.

- Use a Reputable Exchange: Keep your cryptocurrencies on a safe platform with a proven track record.

- Stay informed: The cryptocurrency world is always changing. Keep up with the newest advancements and regulatory changes.

Beyond Bitcoin: The World of Crypto

Bitcoin may be the best-known cryptocurrency, but it is not the only one. Thousands of distinct cryptocurrencies exist, each with its own set of characteristics and objectives. Ethereum, Litecoin, and Ripple are among the most prominent options.

The Future of Cryptography:

The future of cryptocurrencies is unknown. It has the potential to upend the old financial system, but it confronts substantial regulatory and technical challenges. Before joining this complicated and unpredictable market, investors must understand the possible risks and benefits.

Cryptocurrency provides a glimpse of a potentially transformational financial future. However, this is a risky investment. By approaching cryptocurrencies with prudence, completing extensive research, and investing wisely, you might possibly profit from this new asset class as you develop your wealth in the twenty-first century. Remember, cautious investment is essential, and cryptocurrency should be seen as a speculative addition to a well-diversified portfolio.

Conclusion

You've come to the conclusion of your voyage through the wonderful, if often baffling, world of wealth creation in the twenty-first century. This book has given you the information and skills you need to handle the ever-changing financial world. You've looked at both classic and cutting-edge tactics, such as robo-advisors and real estate crowdfunding. Most significantly, you've learnt the value of responsible investment, which is essential for achieving long-term financial stability.

Remember that becoming a billionaire in the twenty-first century is a marathon rather than a sprint. Be patient, disciplined, and continue to educate yourself. By embracing continual learning and using the ideas outlined in this book, you will be well on your way to meeting your financial objectives and constructing a secure future. The future of finance is full with opportunities, and with the correct attitude, you can contribute to its success story. Now, go out and conquer the realm of riches!

www.ingramcontent.com/pod-product-compliance
Lightning Source LLC
Chambersburg PA
CBHW050249230526
45470CB00005B/2187